STEAM MEMORIES: 1950's & 1960's

No.9: SCOTTISH LINES 1

Including: Far North Line, Dundee, Aberdeen & Lines to Wick & Thurso

BOOK LAW PUBLICATIONS

Keith Pirt (on the right) and friends sit beneath the Dornoch station signboard - Thursday 7th July 1955. Note the attire for 1955 railway enthusiasts - polished shoes, trousers with turn-ups, collar and tie, cardigan or waistcoat (optional), and jacket. KRP had a never ending love affair with Scotland and his request to have his ashes spread over the West Highland line was granted and carried out with due ceremony shortly after his passing.

(*previous page*) D40 No.62275 takes charge of a Keith bound goods train at Craigellachie Junction on Tuesday 5th July 1955.

Printed and bound by The Amadeus Press, Cleckheaton, West Yorkshire.
First published in the United Kingdom by Book Law Publications, 382 Carlton Hill, Nottingham, NG4 1JA

INTRODUCTION

Keith Pirt and two companions visited the railways of Scotland, and some of what they had to offer, in the first week of July 1955. This was not Keith's first trip to Scotland, he had managed a short visit in the summer of 1953 but photographic film had not been too plentiful then. The B12 4-6-0s were also coming to the end of their reign on the Great North and the D40 class was still very much intact. The F4 tanks, far from their native pastures, were hanging on at Kittybrewster - just. It was a delightful place - what would 1955 bring?

The itinerary for the 1955 'bash' was quite daunting and involved hundreds of miles of travelling even after they had crossed the border from England. In the first instance, on Saturday 2nd, they struck out westward to Dumfries, looking at the engine shed and station to get themselves started. Then it was off to Stranraer, an outpost and something of a hike either by rail or road. After that it was Ayr, then Ardrossan before calling it a day and getting some rest and refreshment. Engine sheds and stations at all those places were inspected and precious film exposed. Sunday consisted a bash around the Glasgow sheds and because of the number of depots and amount of locomotives therein, photography was hardly used but at St Rollox shed the ex works Highland 0-4-4T No.55053 was given some attention.

Monday morning found the trio in Stirling, or rather at the engine shed and then later at a lineside location just south of the station where trains could be observed and photographed at will. Of course, lineside permits had been requested and granted long beforehand. Having done Stirling the illustrious trio set off for the north and the Highlands calling in at Perth engine shed en route. After stopping to record on film a certain famous summit marker board, the next port of call was Aviemore after which Inverness beckoned with its hostelry, station and engine shed, not necessarily in that order. Over-nighting at Inverness, the refreshed threesome returned on Tuesday morning to the Cairngorms and Boat of Garten station and engine shed. This place was where the first of the former Great North of Scotland 4-4-0s seen during the trip resided temporarily. After that it was off to Keith via Craigellachie Junction and more of the charming D40 class 4-4-0s. Lossiemouth was taken in before Elgin, then it was westward to Forres and later B&B in Inverness again.

Wednesday was another early start along the route of the Far North line to Helmsdale then onward to Thurso and Wick. Returning southward and taking advantage of the long daylight hours of the summer so far north, a stop was made at Tain and then Dingwall before retiring to Inverness (they must have been good digs) for the night.

Thursday 7th July had the trio looking around Inverness engine shed first thing, the overnight arrival of the Highland tank from Glasgow being the focus of their quick excursion to the depot. Then it was back to Dingwall before sampling the delights of the Dornoch branch where the other ex Highland 0-4-4T was working. This was to be their last full day in the Highlands and the weather appears to have been wonderful which, combined with the locations, locomotives and sudden spurts of activity in between long periods of inactivity, made for memorable times.

Aberdeen was their destination on Friday but a quick visit to Inverness shed was made, for a few more pictures, prior to making the journey eastwards. Later that day Kittybrewster and Ferryhill sheds were looked around and once again some gems were waiting, ready and posed for the camera lens. The last day of the trip had soon come around but Saturday was not going to be devoted to travelling home - more important things were on the itinerary. A last look around Kittybrewster revealed just what they wanted. Happy with Aberdeen's offerings, the three travelled south via Forfar shed and Dundee where both the Caley and NBR establishments were inspected. With the sun now dropping rapidly three happy and tired Englishmen crossed the border into England having experienced the delights of rural Scotland before those delights were swept away by the broom of rationalisation and modernisation. Luckily for us, many of those delights have been recorded onto film and here we present some of the images captured during a long hot summer some fifty-three years ago.

The three enthusiasts appear to have travelled through their marathon Scottish journey by motor vehicle mainly due to the fact that the railway timetable would not have made it possible to have put in as many visits and miles as they did manage. Some rail travel seems to have taken place for one or two of the group whilst the car was driven to the trains destination by the third member. This enabled them to sample some of the train journeys and have the flexibility to move on without relying totally on BR.

Keith ventured up to Scotland again later that month, taking in some of the locomotive depots missed on his earlier jaunt - Dalry Road, St Margarets, Thornton Junction, ... - but that's another story.

Looking out for the ancient, rare and short-listed for withdrawal, Keith Pirt started his marathon trek around Scotland at Dumfries where this little gem awaited him and his companions. The ex Caledonian McIntosh '19' class 2P 0-4-4T No.55124 was going about its duties as 'Pilot' at Dumfries station on Saturday 2nd July 1955 unaware of its celebrity status. At this time it was the sole representative of the original ten engines built at St Rollox in 1895 and numbered 19 to 28. The '19' class became the forerunner of a very successful 0-4-4T design, known as the 'Standard Passenger' class, which continued to be developed and built by the CR under McIntosh and later Pickersgill. Even the LMS had ten slightly 'beefed up' versions built by Nasymth Wilson in 1925 so that more than a hundred and twenty went on to serve the LMS, virtually to the end of Grouping. Most lasted into the early 1960's, even No.55124 here managed to eke out a living, albeit on lightweight duties such as this, until October 1961. Having started its career in Glasgow then working its way around various depots in the Central Lowlands such as Airdrie, St Rollox and others, it finished in Dumfries, aged sixty-six - a pensioner indeed and worthy of a photographic record.

Next port of call on that Saturday was Stranraer where the engine shed was visited. This view of the former lifting shop shows a Corkerhill based Stanier Cl.5 No.45036 and a Polmadie based Drummond 2F 0-6-0 No.57238 serviced and ready to work back to Glasgow. The one time Portpatrick & Wigtownshire lifting shop had been converted to a running shed at some time before Grouping and during World War Two its original arched doorways were opened out at the bottom to allow room for engines to stand, as here, half in half out of the shed with adequate room for pedestrian egress. British Railways made the entrances even wider but in so doing had to take out the arches and replace with rolled steel joists but the 30-ton overhead crane in situ. Stranraer motive power depot consisted another shed building, a three-road, through affair, immediately to the south of this shed and just visible on the extreme left. It too was built in local stone with arched entrances which had also been 'opened out' at the bottom by the LMS. Once again BR finished the job properly by providing girders or concrete lintels. This three road shed originally consisted a two-road 'Joint' shed and the one-road Girvan shed from Glasgow & South Western days. To the right is the former Caledonian engine shed which had been closed for many years but retained its arched wooden doors. The LMS had used the place as a store and it remained so until closure of the depot. In the left background a Kingmoor based LMS 2P 4-4-0 No.40615 stands on the centre road of the through shed and looks out onto the 60ft turntable pit which was installed in 1939. Stranraer never really had a large allocation of locomotives with a dozen or so sufficing during BR days but it certainly had a lot of visiting engines which required servicing. To expedite this a simple form of mechanical coal bunker, with a capacity of 25 tons, was erected at the eastern end of the yard. By the end of October 1966 the depot had closed but that event was some eleven years into the future when Keith and his pals recorded this view.

Onwards to Ayr engine shed on this Saturday afternoon, we meet long time 67C resident Sentinel No.47182 having a weekend break from its daily shunting stint at Ayr harbour. For many years this 2-cylinder chain-driven engine carried the title BRITISH RAILWAYS on its bunker sides but when that was eventually removed (after 1952) it was not replaced by the BR crest nor would it have ever received the 'lion and wheel' insignia because seven months after this picture was captured on film it was withdrawn. A long time resident of Ayr shed, perhaps twenty years or more, the 0-4-0 was one of only five such locomotives purchased by the LMS and it was the only one allocated to Scotland, the others working at various periods at Crewe South, St Helens, Preston and Shrewsbury (Clee Hill quarry). Whenever the Sentinel was not available for its early morning job at the docks, a Caley 'Pug' would be drafted in to take its place. Although, apparently, a difficult engine to work - it was idiosyncratic to say the least - the fully enclosed cab made up for its various misdemeanours. In the right background can be seen the wooden coaling stage which served this former G&SW shed until closure to steam in October 1966.

McIntosh '812' class 3F No.57570 was allocated to Hurlford at the time this picture was taken at Ayr shed. It has obviously been refuelled and turned, ready to work home chimney first. Nearly half of Ayr's own locomotive stud consisted of these sturdy Caledonian 0-6-0s, both 2F and 3F types, which worked much of the heavy mineral traffic, usually in pairs, throughout the Ayrshire coalfield. Withdrawn in September 1961, this Neilson Reid built engine was sent to Cowlairs works for scrapping but one of its kind, No.57566, was preserved in its original Caley livery. During the LMS period and into BR days Ayr shed was supplied mainly with steaming coal from two 'local' collieries, Barony and Cronberry Moor. The quality of coal was not to the liking of the deep narrow fireboxes of the Caley 0-6-0s and regular fire cleaning was a necessary occurrence when out on the road. In the background long-time Ayr resident LMS 2P No.40670, still nicely lined, simmers away behind the coal stage. Ayr usually had about ten of the 4-4-0s allocated along with at least four up to half a dozen ex LMS compounds, or 'Compounder' as they were known at 67C.

Also on 67C that afternoon, and keeping the lone Sentinel company, was another Caley 0-6-0 but from a different class and slightly younger than its Hurlford cousin. No.57640 was a McIntosh product but was a member of the '652' class built by the Caledonian Railway at its St Rollox works in June 1908 - note the retro fitted 'LMS' 1908 works plate on the front splasher/sand box. One of three such engines allocated to Ayr shed at the time of KRP's visit, Nos.57633 and 57644 were the other two, and which had been residents long before Nationalisation, two of them from way back into the early 1930's when they were drafted in to replace the time expired Glasgow & South Western 0-6-0 tender engines. The '652' engines were virtually identical to the '812' class but had deeper frames and some detail differences.

LMS Standard classes had been working the former G&SW lines in Scotland since the late 1920's, albeit in small numbers at first but as the withdrawal of the older and non-standard G&SW types grew apace towards the end of that decade the Derby designed 4-4-0 tender engines arrived in ever greater numbers. Vulcan Foundry built Compound No.40908 had started life at the former Caledonian shed at Polmadie, along with a dozen others of its kind in 1927. Ayr shed also got a couple of these new LMS compound engines setting a precedent which was to last nearly thirty years. On 2nd July 1955, with withdrawals having started in earnest, the Ayr allocation consisted just three of the compounds, Nos.40920, 41132, 41155. Long time resident No.41183 had been withdrawn during the previous February. However, 40908 here was by now based at Corkerhill but it too was about to be condemned having been in store at Ayr for some weeks after failing on an incoming passenger train. The engine is still very much intact and has a healthy pile of coal in its tender but it will soon be making a one-way trip to nearby Kilmarnock where the former G&SWR locomotive works was active cutting up withdrawn Scottish Region engines no matter what their origin. The compound would not be out of place at Kilmarnock, the facility there was responsible for cutting up nearly all of the ex LMS 4-4-0s resident in Scotland - 40908's turn took place during February 1956.

Ardrossan was the last depot visited by KRP and friends on Saturday 2nd July 1955. The weather managed to stay dry and the light conditions were to be expected. Only one picture was taken at 67D - this resident and fairly clean ex LMS 2P being the subject. Ardrossan had about fourteen of these engines on its books at that time but none of the 4P compounds though three of the 4P's had been resident at Ardrossan from new in 1927 until about 1930. The depot was not responsible for any of the long distance main line passenger work except the Largs to Glasgow business trains and the boat trains from that place. These were easily within the capabilities of the 2P with their large coupled wheels. No.40638 was put into traffic from Crewe works in August 1931, initially to Corkerhill shed. It went later to Ayr and was sent to Ardrossan during the BR period. Withdrawn from Stranraer shed in May 1962, it was sold for scrap May 1963 to West of Scotland Shipbreaking Co. at Troon. Like Ayr shed, Ardrossan had been built inside a triangle of lines west of Ardrossan (Town) station. The G&SWR had established the depot here in late 1894 with a shed containing four through roads. The coaling stage was an elevated structure where manual coaling was required and which continued until the shed was closed to steam in 1965. The last 2P to leave, in January 1962, was No.40578 which, appropriately perhaps, had been the first of the class allocated to Ardrossan in 1928. The shed itself was in use until about 1969 when diesels were serviced. After complete closure the place was used to store dozens of the unreliable and redundant Clayton Type 1 diesel locomotives during the early 1970's. However, back in 1955 the ex LMS 2P 4-4-0s were still highly regarded by the Southwestern' enginemen and they were looked after as well as any good steed.

On Monday 4th July 1955 KRP and companions arrived in Stirling having spent Sunday 'shed bashing' Glasgow. There was no rest day, Sabbath or not. Stirling station offered up ex LMS and ex LNER types but the first locomotive captured that morning was BR Standard Class 5 No.73009 negotiating the trackwork at the south end of the station after the Stirling stop with an express from Dundee to Glasgow (Buchanan Street). The Perth based 4-6-0, complete with tablet exchanger on the cab side, appears to be in a fairly clean state, as do the BR MK.1 coaches behind. Note the vacuum standpipe on the bufferbeam is placed much higher than was normal for this class. The reason behind this extra height was to enable the 63A Standards, Nos.73005 to 73009 and also Polmadie's Nos.73055 to 73064 to be fitted with large snowploughs, the attachment of which relied heavily on the bottom edge of the bufferbeam being clear. Besides No.73009 carrying the Manson tablet exchanger, for single line working, Nos.73005 to 73008, 73077 and 73078 are also believed to have been fitted with such catchers at different periods. A similar apparatus, the Whitaker automatic type, was fitted to many of the class working over the Somerset & Dorset Joint. No.73009 spent most of its working life allocated to Perth shed from July 1951 to January 1963 when it moved south to Corkerhill. It spent another three and a half years working from the former G&SW depot before being withdrawn in July 1966. It was sold for scrap two months later. 11

Not too long afterwards, Stanier Cl.5 No.45389 passed Keith's position (a trackside photographic permit had been obtained well in advance of this visit) as it headed south with a slightly heavier express - THE BON ACCORD. Another of Perth's huge allocation of Cl.5's, No.45389 was in dire need of a good clean, its employment on this prestige train was perhaps as a substitute for a failed 'booked' engine? The 4-6-0 had arrived at Perth during wartime from Bath. In May 1957 it moved to Stirling and spent the next eight years there before withdrawal in April 1965. In the station an unidentified engine has drawn up to a platform with a southbound working.

Next along was former North British Railway 'Glen', LNER D34 class No.62484 GLEN LYON working a two-coach ordinary passenger train. Arriving from St Margarets shed in August 1953, this engine was to be based at Perth until October 1960 when it retreated to former home territory at Thornton. Meanwhile, down at the station further trains have appeared and are awaiting their turn to head south. It was a busy place Stirling in 1955 - glorious.

The last of the Stirling trains observed was this southbound working with another Perth Cl.5, No.44931 storming out of the station past the gasworks. The driver is keeping an eye on the photographers and must have been reading their minds. He co-operated nicely by darkening the sky.

Continuing our journey northwards, our next stop was Perth where the engine shed beckoned. Ex Caledonian Pickersgill 3P No.54467 posed for the camera in the shed yard where it was performing shed pilot duties moving loaded coal wagons over to the coaling plant recharge hopper. Note the shunting pole straddling the front footplate. Just short of its fortieth birthday, this North British Loco. Co. built 4-4-0 had been a long time resident of 63A along with eight others of its kind but in November 1955 it moved over to Forfar shed where it spent its remaining years prior to withdrawal in October 1959. To the end these engines were dual-fitted with both Westinghouse and vacuum brakes.

Coaled, watered, turned and ready to head home, visiting St Margarets J37 No.64572 had recently undergone a General overhaul at Inverurie works - 6th May to 3rd June - and looks all the better for it. Another NBL product, entering traffic in August 1918, it was to have nine more years working life before it when captured on film during this July day in 1955. The same could not be said for the resident ex LMS compound in the background with its smokebox door gaping open. Having been allocated to Perth shed for most of its existence, it was now awaiting attention of sorts but was deemed unserviceable. Four months later, in November, it was condemned. By early 1956 it was at Kilmarnock works queuing up for the scrapman with other ex LMS 4-4-0s. The economical life of the average steam locomotive was reckoned to be thirty years but No.40921 only attained 28 such years. Still, what was a couple of years when future British Railways steam locomotives were lucky to attain eight years working life before the meaning of economy was lost in an avalanche of modernisation and corporate waste.

It is amazing how many of the former Caley engines managed to keep hold of their Westinghouse air brakes for so long. This McIntosh '439' class 2P 0-4-4T was yet another with the equipment in July 1955. Although the air-braked rolling stock had ceased to exist many years before Nationalisation, it was decided to keep the equipment for engine braking where already fitted rather than change over to steam braking. The train braking being performed by the vacuum ejector. We are still at Perth engine shed having moved further into the yard. Resident No.55218 was one of the smaller inhabitants of 63A but had been around the place for the whole of the BR period having arrived at some time during the LMS era. These four-coupled tanks (there were over a dozen of them at Perth and its subs) were used on the many branch lines once criss-crossing this area of Scotland. Built at St Rollox in June 1913, this engine worked until January 1960 when withdrawal took place.

Druimuachdar Pass Summit 1484 feet above sea level. Monday afternoon, 4th July 1955. It was always worthwhile waiting here at the lineside for trains working their way up to the summit, albeit frequency did not match the grandeur. Although the main road was immediately behind you it was isolated enough to be quiet so that you could hear trains coming from the south or north when they were still some miles away. Although the former Highland Railway main line between Stanley Junction and Culloden Moor is nearly all single track, the section between Blair Atholl and Dalwhinnie consists Up and Down lines so it was possible - if you were lucky enough - to get one train passing from south to north shortly before a north to south working passed. Nearly always the trains were double-headed and heavy, sometimes they were banked from Blair Atholl. Stanier Class 5's dominated the motive power pool on the line during late LMS and BR days but so what. To see a pair of steam locomotives working extremely hard whilst seemingly not making much headway, and blackening the sky to boot, is still a sight to behold - and a memory to cherish. The sign board looks a little weather beaten but its anchorage appears solid enough - oh yes, windy episodes up here can be somewhat daunting not to mention the rain, and as for the snow.....

Aviemore shed was the next location visited on that Monday. It was getting late now and a dash to Inverness for refreshment and rest beckoned. The former Highland engine shed at Aviemore consisted four covered dead-end roads, built in local stone with arched doorways, and a central vented ridge. A elevated coaling stage at the south end of the yard was accompanied by a turntable. Opened in 1898 for the inauguration of the new direct line services to Inverness via Carr Bridge and Moy, the shed remained in use by steam locomotives until July 1962 when a couple of diesel shunters sheltered there. By 1966 BR had given the place up, at least for locomotive purposes but the yard was rented to a small private enterprise. In 1975 the Strathspey Railway acquired the site and returned the place to its former glory, housing locomotives and rolling stock. Here in July 1955, former Caledonian Pickersgill 4-4-0 3P No.54488, a 'local' at 60B, is stabled on the road beside the shed. Note the engine pits in the foreground and the clean state of the yard. There were at least four of these ex CR 3P 4-4-0s working from Aviemore by 1950 along with an 0-6-0 and an 0-4-4T from the south but in 1955 only two of the 3P's, Nos 54466 and 54488 remained. The ex Highland engines had all but disappeared by 1950 hence the influx of CR types.

Boat of Garten, Tuesday 5th July. Having spent the night at Inverness, the trio ventured over to this western outpost of the erstwhile Great North of Scotland Railway in order to cram as much of this pre-Group company into the day. Their first encounter was D40 No.62268 at Boat of Garten shed. The Keith based 4-4-0 was here for the week working the branch passenger services to Craigellachie, whilst goods work was being performed by another 61C D40 No.62267 and ex Caley 3F 0-6-0 No.57634 from Inverness. Note the far from home territory Western Region 13-ton open wagon (W131731) being used to store the grounded ash and clinker. By the looks of things it will take a number of wagons and squad of cleaners to get rid of the pile between the 4-4-0 and the wagon.

The Inverness engine takes water after turning and is ready to work back home over the old Highland route via Dava and Forres. The 3F was no stranger to this area having been allocated to nearby Aviemore for a number of years since the war. During the 1954 summer it was used almost exclusively on the Speyside passenger services between Boat of Garten and Craigellachie, the usual D40 being in short supply for some reason. The tall structure to the right of the 0-6-0 is something of a mystery to this writer but it certainly had a purpose. The body is made up of a debarked tree trunk and has a fabricated steel bracket at its top. A chain hangs from either end of the bracket and is connected to what appears to be a winding handle secured by another bracket near the bottom of the pole. The chain is secured to itself by a ring of sorts just above the winding handle. Could it be some sort of crude crane for lifting what?

A nice view of Boat of Garten engine shed with 62268 and 57634 taking a break from the daily toil. The Great North of Scotland Railway built this shed at the western extremity of their system in 1866. Replacing an earlier, similar establishment at Nethy Bridge, it was situated slightly north of the junction station, to the east side of the line from Craigellachie. As can be seen, it was substantially constructed in local stone with arched entrances to the two roads. Along its eastern side was a turntable, access to which was gained via the road by the water tower and coaling platform. A sub shed of Keith for most of its existence, it became a sub of Aviemore in BR days but its motive power was still supplied by Keith. Closed in November 1958, the shed stood empty for a number of years before demolition in 1961. However, during its time of disuse especially, the shed housed the former Highland Railway 4-4-0 BEN ALDER inside, and later outside when the shed roof became unsafe. The 'Ben' was actually inside the shed on this date awaiting a call for preservation which, as we all regret, never came. Further to the mystery pole in the previous illustration, this view has now revealed a second similar pole sited nearer to the shed and alongside the line used for the platelayers trolley. Were these two poles used in conjunction with each other to lift rail from the trolley? The evidence is stacking up on the ground.

Having just handed over the key to the signal bobby (note the tablet catcher in front of the signal box steps), the fireman of Stanier Class 5 No.45136 looks towards the camera as his mixed goods train comes off the single line section from Forres. At this time the Class 5 was allocated to Aviemore, its second stint at that depot. Coming into traffic in May 1935 at Patricroft shed as No.5136, the 4-6-0 started its move northwards in September 1937 when it was allocated to Upperby. In 1942 it moved on to Perth but was not long there before being sent onto the Highland Section and reallocating to Aviemore in October 1942. With it came No.5138. In November 1945 it moved to Inverness followed by 5138 seven months later. In October 1952 No.45136 was sent back to Aviemore from where it worked until July 1960. Its services no longer required, it moved on to Perth, the whole of the Highland area by now becoming rapidly dieselised. It was withdrawn in October 1964 as redundant to requirements. Here, however, in July 1955 it will shortly shunt the station and pick-up wagons ready for southbound passage. In the meantime D40 No.62268 backs down to the station for its next duty - it was suddenly getting quite busy.

Nicely coupled up to its two-coach train, No.62268 is made ready for its eastward departure. In the background the Aviemore Cl.5 is busy picking up wagons to add to its train which was left stabled in the station.

A panoramic view of Boat of Garten station and its goods yard, looking west towards Aviemore. No.62268 gets away to Craigellachie whilst the Stanier 4-6-0 continues sorting out the wagons for its southbound train. The station nameboard reads: **BOAT OF GARTEN** JUNCTION - CHANGE FOR SPEYSIDE LINE. The three posters decorating the end of the timber built platform facilities are extolling the virtues of, from left to right: Culzean Castle; The Yorkshire Coast; Aberdeen. Below those, the Virol enamelled sign states that 'School Children Need It'. The station here opened on Monday 3rd August 1863 although the GNSR did not arrive until August 1866 when the place became a Joint station. The whole station, including the goods facilities, closed on Monday 18th October 1965 but before then British Railways had removed the pitched roof of the waiting shed and replaced it with a simple inclined roof, even the chimneys disappeared - and no doubt the welcoming open fires - whilst at the same time the building itself was shortened by about a third of its original length - it had the appearance of a bus shelter with doors. On the Down, northbound platform, just out of picture to the right, a much larger building incorporated the booking hall, staff rooms and further waiting rooms. That building was mainly constructed of timber and managed to reach closure without too many changes. Happily, preservation in the shape of the Strathspey Railway has brought some of the former life back into the 'junction'. May it prosper as long as the original establishment.

25

A mad dash to Craigellachie by road found the branch engine, D40 No.62268, already being serviced by its crew. The junction here was pure GNSR, with the line to Aberdeen heading out to the south towards Dufftown where it turned north-east to Keith to make a junction with the Highland Railway. From there, where the HR advance eastwards stopped, the GNSR took a torturous route south-eastwards to Aberdeen. Northwards from Craigellachie the line headed towards Elgin where another junction with the Highland was encountered. The GNSR split just north of Elgin and went immediately north to Lossiemouth or you could go east along the coastal route as far as Tillynaught where another junction was made for the short branch to Banff. Carrying on southwards you would meet up with the Keith line via a wye junction going to either Grange or Cairnie Junction. On this Tuesday in July 1955 it was nice to savour something of the old Great North of Scotland which is long gone. Note the mixture of timber and stone in the architecture. Never a very prosperous company, the GNSR made do with what was available. It can be seen that the water tank had recently been elevated higher by the addition of seven further courses of stone to the original plinth. For a station which did not generate a lot of revenue at the best of times, expensive building work must have been a great strain on finances.

D40 No.62275 SIR DAVID STEWART joined No.62268 on the servicing road as the latter was actually on the turntable ready to turn for forward running back towards Boat of Garten. No.62275 had called in for water whilst working a goods train to Keith from Elgin. Once its thirst was sated it returned to its train and carried on its journey. By the end of the year it will have been condemned - 20th December. It was cut up at Inverurie at the end of March 1956 leaving just six members of the class intact. Not that the original brass nameplate fixed in 1920 has disappeared to be replaced by a parsimonious painted version - very NBR. The 'namer' was one of the superheated versions of the class, in fact only those with names were superheated, the rest had saturated boilers.

Following the Keith bound goods train to its destination the gallant trio head further east and meet K2 No.61734 outside Keith engine shed. This 'old-timer' had been at Keith since the previous July and was to spend another year at 61C before withdrawal aged 42 years. Since coming into traffic in April 1914 this 2-6-0 had been allocated to sheds on either the GN main line or on former Great Eastern lines. Its move to Scotland took place as late as June 1951 when it went to Eastfield. Eight months later it went over to Dunfermline then, after a major overhaul at Cowlairs, on to Thornton Junction shed before arriving in Aberdeen during May 1953. When this picture was recorded the K2 class was still intact but the start of withdrawals was only three months away. Keith was blessed with two engine sheds up to 1948 when the former Inverness & Aberdeen Junction (HR) shed at the west end of the joint station was closed by BR. Facilities were then centred on the 1856 built GNSR shed which stood east of the station on the south side of the line. This shed consisted four dead-end roads, was stone built with arch doorways and in need of renovation. The resultant changes can be seen behind the K2 in this view and were carried out in 1953 when steel girders replaced the arches and new brickwork was built above them whilst the building was re-roofed. Closure to steam traction took place in January 1961 but diesels used the place until the early 70's. The town was likewise blessed with two stations, the junction/joint station and another GNSR station originally known Earlsmill but renamed Keith Town in 1897, which was situated west of the junction. That place closed in May 1968 - no doubt at the top of Beeching's GNS closure list.

On 21st April 1908 the Highland Railway and the Great North of Scotland Railway commenced through running for their Aberdeen-Inverness passenger services. To enable the GNSR engines to handle the HR stock three D40's were equipped with vacuum ejectors and they were then able to run through to Inverness with Highland stock. Likewise an equal number of HR 4-4-0s were fitted with Westinghouse brakes to enable them to work through to Aberdeen with GNSR stock. D40 No.62262 was one of the original three fitted in 1908 and was obviously a regular visitor to the Capital of the Highlands - Inverness. Seen on 5th July 1955 at Keith Junction, carrying the 'Keith No.1' target board, the D40 is reduced to working the station pilot - a far cry from the heady days when it hauled the premier trains on the GNSR. All of the class except No.62278 HATTON CASTLE retained their Westinghouse equipment for engine braking and operating the sanding gear. Train braking was by vacuum ejector. The 'odd one out' had a steam brake fitted for engine braking whilst sanding was also by steam. At the end of the 1955 summer timetable No.62262 would be laid up and then condemned; it was one of nine of the class withdrawn that year.

Lossiemouth was the next venue and here, at the station throat, we have ex Caley 0-4-4T No.55221 (note the newly acquired stove-pipe chimney), the branch engine from Elgin, moving down the platform to couple-up for the return working to Elgin. The 2P tank engine was a long way from its former stamping ground around Glasgow and was now allocated to Keith, sub-shedded to Elgin, but it would be around a lot longer than the D40 4-4-0s it replaced on these duties finally being withdrawn in October 1961. The station here was opened in August 1852 and as part of the Beeching cuts, was closed on Monday 6th April 1964. Latterly, a couple of former LMS corridor coaches formed the rolling stock of the branch train, the erstwhile GNSR stock having been withdrawn for some time. Way back in early LNER days Ramsay MacDonald lived at Lossiemouth and a through sleeping car service was introduced between King's Cross, Elgin and Lossiemouth. This ran until 1939 and at first comprised a first class vehicle but later a it was made up by a composite twin when third class sleeping cars were introduced. Note that in this July 1955 view, with another nine years of operation, the station appears to be well looked after in its situation by the sea - the two times Prime Minster would have been justly proud of the station in 1955 as he probably was in the 20's and 30's.

On to Elgin now where D40 No.62269 was acting as 'Elgin No.1' station pilot prior to moving back to Aberdeen in August for its final days before being condemned on 9th September. The end was certainly 'on the cards' for this engine. Its last boiler change had been at a General overhaul at Inverurie in May 1951 when it got the boiler from withdrawn D41 No.62227. However, in this view the 4-4-0 looks healthy enough and has one of the tender cabs for use on branch lines where engine turning was not possible due to lack of turntables. No.62264, the penultimate D40, took over the Elgin pilot job from No.62269 in August. It too had a tender cab but it was of the wooden variety whereas our 4-4-0 here has the steel plate version. Note the former LMS coaching stock in the background.

Gainfully employed No.62269 goes about the business of shunting at Elgin. Besides the out of use signals, note also the new 16-ton mineral wagons on the right - these keep cropping up during our journey.

Last call of the day on the Tuesday was to Forres. Forres was the original junction of the line from Perth to Inverness (the old route) and the Inverness & Aberdeen line to Elgin. The Inverness & Perth Railway opened an engine shed here in August 1863. Seen as the background to this photograph, the shed consisted two roads and was substantially built from stone with arched entrances, topped with a pitched roof. About 1901 the gable end with the two openings was taken down and replaced by a wooden screen which sufficed until the shed was closed to steam by BR in May 1959. Ex Caledonian Railway 3F 0-6-0T No.56301 was one of seven locomotives allocated to 60E, as British Railways had coded the place then, all of which had no Highland connections at all coming from the CR via the LMS and BR after World War Two. On this July day in 1955 the seven engines concerned were 3P 4-4-0 Nos.54471, 54472, 54473 (arrived pre 1/1/48), 54482; 2P 0-4-4T No.55178; 3F 0-6-0T No.56301; 3F 0-6-0 No.57620 (both arrived pre 1/1/48). The allocation in September 1935 was very different with only Highland engines about the place: 2P 4-4-0 Nos.14398, 14399, 14400, 14401, 14402, 14406, 14422; 4P 0-6-4T No.15300; LMS 3F 0-6-0T No.16623.

Forres solitary 'Caley' 2P, or 2PT acording to the legend on the cabside, appears rather clean as were most of the depot's charges that day. Stanier Cl.5 No.45463 of Perth was also on shed but had the usual coating of grime.

On Wednesday 6th July the trek north to Wick and Thurso began and the first stop was at Helmsdale (population 691. Distance from London 669 miles) where Inverness based Cl.5 No.44991 was being watered during the station stop on the way to Wick. The wooden engine shed with its Dutch barn type roof sits snugly alongside the station. In 1871 this place was the terminus of the line from Inverness and would remain so until the line was completed to Wick in July 1874. Conveniently situated about half way between Wick and Inverness, Helmsdale became a locomotive and crew change over point and remained as such until LMS days. With the coming of the Stanier Cl.5 in 1935 only crews changed over, with the Inverness crew taking the next southbound working from Wick. Prior to that the Inverness and Wick enginemen worked lodging turns and for this Helmsdale was equipped with a dormitory in the shape of an old coach. Helmsdale meanwhile maintained a reasonable allocation up to 1960 when the Dornoch branch closed and diesels were introduced to the Highland lines. The shed closed in 1961. The coal stack here was so old that wild plants and weeds had taken refuge on what remained of its flat top surface. Inside the shed long time resident No.57587 an ex 'Caley' 3F 0-6-0 hides in the gloom.

Another Helmsdale resident was ex CR 3P 4-4-0 No.54495 which was used for assisting trains up some of the steeper climbs. Here more mundane duties are being performed as coal stage/shed pilot. The 60ft turntable was a recent addition to the facilities at 60C and was installed in 1948 to replace a 55ft appliance. This one was equipped with a vacuum tractor and made life at Helmsdale a lot easier for the shed staff. A coaling crane, seen above the 3P's cab, was another mechanical aid. However, for all Helmsdale's importance either in HR, LMS or BR days, the shed remained as a timber structure, the Highland made do twice with the remains of the first shed after natural catastrophes. The LMS spent millions on renewing and modernising engine sheds up and down the country, as did BR but only the expenditure of the new turntable was accredited to Helmsdale in recent times. The original roof was a single pitch affair which the gales slowly took to pieces. A second roof was put on about 1899 followed by the Dutch barn type after another severe storm in 1921. Constant maintenance has kept the roof in good order into the BR period. Obviously nobody saw any reason to invest too much into this location.

Between Kildonan and Kinbrace was one of those request stops with a waiting shelter built in typical Highland style with style. This was Borrobol Platform as seen from a northbound train. Note the two-way signal and more especially the unguarded counterweight arms. It seems the signals were permanently 'pulled-off' so there was no movement to cause injury or damage to members of the public and where were the counterweights? Brought into use as a platform in 1880, this place had been a 'stop by request' from September 1876, probably with a ladder in use for intending passengers. The platform closed at the end of November 1965.

Forty-six miles further on from Helmsdale we come to Georgemas Junction, Caithness, where the line to Thurso headed off westward from the mainlines easterly heading. We are looking down from the footbridge in a westerly direction, the main line from Helmsdale coming in from the left and the branch to Thurso going off to the right. This station opened with the line in July 1874 and originally, as here, had extensive goods facilities including a 1-ton capacity crane.

It appears that livestock was one of the main revenue earners on the line, although seasonal, with sheep accounting for nearly all of the movements. Georgemas Junction is still open to passenger traffic, as are most of the stations in this isolated corner of the British Isles. During World War One, from 1916 to be precis, the whole of northern Scotland, north of Inverness and the Great Glen, was made into a restricted area, the military installations therein being of such importance to the nation that nobody was allowed in without a permit.

The Thurso branch passenger engine at the head of its two-coach train in July 1955. Once again the Caledonian rules - just. This is McIntosh 2P No.55236 the last numbered member of the '439' class and which came into traffic in the last month before Grouping. Allocated to 60D Wick and its sub shed Thurso by July 1955, the 0-4-4T had been resident at the former G&SW shed at Hurlford on the eve of Nationalisation and before that, still in Southwestern' country at Beith. In the summer following this scene being recorded, it transferred south (there was nowhere further north) to Inverness and its place on the Thurso job was taken by a Stanier 2-6-2T No.40150 which, apparently, was never liked. In the twenty-odd miles between Wick and Thurso there used to be, including Georgemas Junction, five intermediate stations but with the exception of the junction station here they are all closed, most on that fateful day of 13th June 1960 when the axe fell on so many of the former Highland Railway stations, halts and branch lines. One place, however, the next stop for this train here, Hoy Halt, managed to survive until the end of November 1965.

Thurso, the most northerly terminus, railway station, engine shed, goods yard, signal box, railway installation - call it what you like - in Britain. 722 miles from London (Euston). Population 4,278 in 1952. Opened as a railway terminus on Tuesday, 28th July 1874 and still doing business as such. The railway station had a road link with Scrabster harbour from where sailing's linked the mainland to the Orkney Isles and still do (add the Faeroes too for good measure). This magnificent view of Wednesday 6th July 1955 captures the whole railway installation and some of the surrounding town. Note the large amount of goods rolling stock seemingly jamming up the passenger station, besides the goods yard. Wick and Georgemas Junction passenger trains were using the left, uncovered, side of the platform at this time. No doubt the season had something to do with that reasoning. The place is reminiscent of what can be found at a preserved railway site today rather than a semi-thriving 'back of beyond' terminal area - it appears to be very modellable. The engine shed had lost its 52ft turntable during the previous couple of years, the outline of the pit is just discernible to the left of the water tower where the points are installed for the empty wagon road in front of the shed. When the turntable was still available, 4-4-0 tender engines were used to run the passenger service from Wick and the junction but tank engines with enclosed cabs became necessary upon its removal hence the 'Caley' tank and later incumbents, although ex CR 4-4-0 No.54439 was often in use during the summer of 1955. The shed itself is just as it was built - solid, sturdy, unmoving - only white paint around the archway had been added at some point during the early BR years. The interior was apparently immaculately whitewashed too, its resident locomotives not requiring shelter until late into the night and therefore having less time to pollute the place.

Off to Wick next where the engine shed appeared to be busy and somewhat crowded, the Stanier Cl.5 dominating the place as it had done for virtually the last two decades. Standing abreast, left to right, are No.44991 which was seen at Helmsdale earlier in the day, No.44992, and then a grubby looking (they all were really) No.44785 (reportedly the last Cl.5 - steam locomotive to work off Wick shed). A motorised Permanent Way machine is being inspected on the breakdown crane road whilst on the extreme right washing flaps in the breeze on the propped-up line - how very homely. The one-time messroom, in the guise of a timber hut, is now used as a wood store for fire lighting, the pile outside giving a fair idea of how much of that activity went on at Wick. The two road shed was another of the 1874 Highland strongholds built to last a hundred years. It was a through road type building with a turntable at its eastern end. Intense wartime activity brought modernisation in the shape of a 25-ton capacity mechanical coal bunker but that apparently was all. Peacetime saw the return of normality and investment passed by without stopping except for a new roof requirement in 1959. After closure the place did manage its centenary though and was last reported as 'in use as a supermarket' - the HR Directors would have been proud of that fact and that their vision of building a railway line so far to the north of mainland Britain was still a viable one. Although small compared with most railway installations during the age of steam, the outpost at Wick had to be self-sufficient in many things. Besides the motive power and spare engines, the place had, as already noted, its breakdown gang with crane and vans, a permanent way gang, a more than ample supply of coal and much more besides including a dedicated work force.

Ex CR 3P 4-4-0 No.54491 worked out its last decade of life at Wick, along with three others of its kind and an 0-6-0 goods engine also of Caley origin. They also saw the end of steam in this part of the world, one of the first parts of British Railways to be fully dieselised. Note that, even in 1955, lining has been omitted from the livery of this one time express passenger locomotive. In September 1935 Wick engine shed could boast the following locomotives on its allocation: 3P 4-6-0 Nos.14681, 14683; 0P 0-4-4T No.15053 (with 15051 at Lybster); 3F 0-6-0 Nos.17694, 17701. The Stanier Cl.5 was already entrenched at Inverness and by the autumn of 1935 were daily visitors to Wick along with the remnants of the old Highland classes still extant at Dingwall and Helmsdale. Thurso at this time had 2P 4-4-0 No.14415.

Our final look at Wick gives us this view of the station with one of Keith's friends posing alongside Cl.5 No.44785 at the head of the late afternoon departure to Inverness. The Cl.5 'inside' is not recorded but it had a riveted tender to may well have been No.44992. Wick station was unchanged from its opening day in 1874 and the town's population had not changed that much - its population circa 1950, was 11,322 souls. Although further from London, by train, than Thurso at 729 miles, it was situated further east and some fourteen miles south-east of Georgemas Junction so that the former place could rightly claim its isolation. Note, once again, how clean and uncluttered the platform was. The remains of the closed $13^1/_2$ mile long Lybster branch were not inspected on this trip but apparently the course of the route was still unmistakable, years after the track had been lifted following closure in April 1944. Most of the buildings are intact except the engine shed at Lybster which was demolished some years ago.

With the evening sun casting long shadows over the eastern shore of Ross & Cromarty, Tain engine shed presents its front face, complete with resident 4-4-0 No.54496. situated south-east of the station, the shed stood on the east side of the line. Here we are looking south-east towards Dingwall. Another substantial building in stone, it was erected in the winter of 1877 after the previous wooden structure had burnt down earlier that year. There had been a wooden engine shed at Tain since the summer of 1864 but that shed had become a victim of the railway's advancement to the north so it was shifted to Invergordon prior to returning to Tain in 1874. In BR days Tain was a sub-shed of Helmsdale and on this July evening in 1955 the stabled 4-4-0 was on the strength of Inverness. This establishment closed in June 1962. The station, serving a local populace of 2,422 people, is still open.

The last call of the day was at Dingwall where the Wick-Inverness train, with No.44785 at the head, was encountered as it entered the single line section south of the station (note the signalman ready to pass the staff). Having covered over 140 miles already, and made numerous stops en route, the train has only eighteen more miles to its destination. Likewise the three amigos who have covered nearly four hundred miles themselves, making numerous stops for photographs, etc. It had been a long day but we will return here tomorrow.

One of the two motive power relics of the Highland Railway still extant in 1955 was this diminutive home-built 0-4-4 tank engine which was surviving through work on the Dornoch branch along with a sister engine. No.55053 was one of four such engines built during 1905-6 at the Highland's Lochgorm locomotive works on the other side of the main line from the engine shed - they were in fact the last locomotives to be built at that factory. Classified 'W' by the HR and numbered 25, 40, 45 and 46 by them, the four were renumbered by the LMS. Nos.15052(40) and 15054(46) did not make it into British Railways ownership being withdrawn in 1930 and 1945 respectively. They worked the Lybster Light Railway from Wick. The two survivors, now numbered 55051(25) and 55053(45) were not withdrawn until July 1956 and January 1957 respectively. No.55053 managed six further months life because of an overhaul carried out at St Rollox works during May and June 1955, when its boiler was refurbished. Here, on Thursday 7th July, we see the engine being stabled at Inverness shed after arriving back from Glasgow the night before. Restored to full BR lined black livery, the little tank will be taken back to Helmsdale once its boiler had been washed out, fire lit, steam raised and all the necessary checks have been carried out.

Giving the 0-4-4T a push into a stall, the wee 'Pug' No.56011 was paused on the turntable so that Keith and friends could record the moment on film. The staff at Inverness shed were such obliging folk, as were most of the motive power staff throughout the Highlands.

In September 1935 this ex CR Pickersgill 3P was stationed at St Rollox in Glasgow but by the eve of Nationalisation it was allocated to the greener pastures offered by Inverness and found plenty of employment working over the main lines radiating out to all points of the compass from the Highland headquarters. The engine could be in Wick one day, Perth the next, then off to Kyle of Lochalsh perhaps, and Keith on the following day - variety indeed. When captured at Inverness shed in July 1955, it was resting after working in from Forres, its then home depot. The 4-4-0 was thirty-five years old and had given value to its three separate owners. Indeed BR would get almost another seven years out of its before it went for scrap in 1962. Just look at that large lump of stone behind - shades of the Euston arch especially in its demise!

Dingwall, Ross & Cromarty - 586 miles from London. Population 2,551. Weather on Thursday 7th July 1955, sunny with occasional cloud, light wind, warm. Subject in view - the engine shed. Situated at the south end of the station, this structure was opened a long ago as 1870 during the two-pronged drive north and west by the Highland. Built in timber, when the HR finances were stretching once again building the new lines, it is a wonder the place survived so long without incident. Certainly none were recorded but renewal must have taken place to certain components such as the roof, cladding, smoke vents (the latter certainly were replaced pre-war according to photographic evidence). Anyway, the place survived intact for such a long time in one of the most wind and storm swept areas of the British Isles. A sub of Inverness, it tended to keep hold of the same engines for many years, as long as Inverness kept them on the books. No.54458, lazily smoking outside the shed and limbering up for some work, was one of the McIntosh 3P 4-4-0s allocated to 60A and which at the end of the LMS was stationed at Perth (it was at Stirling pre-war) as though waiting to spring northwards in the quest of gentle, more rural work in the Highlands. These 4-4-0s spent much of their time at Dingwall banking trains over the Kyle line to Raven's Rock (458 feet a.s.l.) between Achterneed and Garve. On the left, shunting a lone wagon, is another ex Caledonian engine, McIntosh 2P 0-4-4T No.55199, a long time resident of this place. Closed like most other Highland Region engine sheds, in 1961, the last occupant of this shed was an ex Western Region pannier tank No.1649 which, in July of that year, became station pilot!

Further north on that Thursday, at The Mound we meet the other Dornoch branch tank engine No.55051 which was taking care of business all on its own whilst sister 55053 was away at works. The decision by KRP and his two companions to visit the Dornoch branch was a good one because the two Highland 0-4-4 tank engines would not be working the line for many more years. This engine looks to be both tired and worn out and it had not been near main works since 1949, the owners title still adorning the tank side nearly seven years after it was superseded by the BR crest. Behind the tank engine, the firebox of a Stanier Class 5 which is heading a northbound train on the main line, can be made out. Junction for the branch to Dornoch and opened in April 1868, this station closed in June 1960, when the branch itself was closed. At Nationalisation there was about forty-two intermediate stations and platforms between Inverness and Wick plus a private platform. Nowadays there are still twenty-two stations, eleven of which have passing loops, which is a fairly good reflection of the importance of the railway to this area of Scotland.

The view of the start of the Dornoch branch from The Mound station. Curving away across the small viaduct which spans the waters of Loch Fleet, the branch turns south towards Dornoch some seven and three-quarter miles away.

Mound Rock which gave the junction station its name, looks out over Loch Fleet and towers above the railway junction. The station buildings and water tank can be seen poking out through the trees to the left of the viaduct. The stone and steel viaduct was, however, in need of strengthening and one pier in particular can be seen to have had some bracing added.

Making its way now to Dornoch on this Thursday, the little 0-4-4T has charge of the mixed branch train near Cambusavie. Apparently, one run each way was mixed with goods vehicles. In 1955 the stations on the line, including the three intermediate stations, Cambusavie (actually a request halt), Skelbo, and Embo, were given revamps, the platforms at the last two mentioned places plus Dornoch terminus platform, were all rebuilt. The permanent way along certain stretches of the branch had also been refreshed, not so the fencing just here. All this work and expenditure usually meant (in the BR period) that a line or station was about to be closed within the next year or so, the accountants using the high figures of the refurbishment against the low income from the traffic. The Dornoch branch managed to survive another five years before the end inevitably came.

Having run round its mixed train at Dornoch terminus, No.55051 is now marshalling and sorting some goods wagons into the platform line. The single passenger vehicle used in the train at this time in July 1955 was BCK SC6703M which always had a van coupled for the parcels traffic.

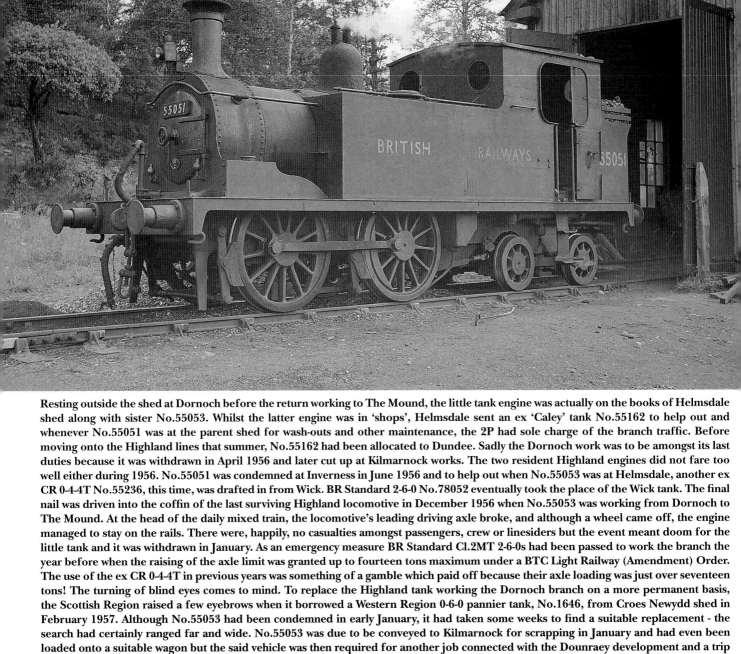

Resting outside the shed at Dornoch before the return working to The Mound, the little tank engine was actually on the books of Helmsdale shed along with sister No.55053. Whilst the latter engine was in 'shops', Helmsdale sent an ex 'Caley' tank No.55162 to help out and whenever No.55051 was at the parent shed for wash-outs and other maintenance, the 2P had sole charge of the branch traffic. Before moving onto the Highland lines that summer, No.55162 had been allocated to Dundee. Sadly the Dornoch work was to be amongst its last duties because it was withdrawn in April 1956 and later cut up at Kilmarnock works. The two resident Highland engines did not fare too well either during 1956. No.55051 was condemned at Inverness in June 1956 and to help out when No.55053 was at Helmsdale, another ex CR 0-4-4T No.55236, this time, was drafted in from Wick. BR Standard 2-6-0 No.78052 eventually took the place of the Wick tank. The final nail was driven into the coffin of the last surviving Highland locomotive in December 1956 when No.55053 was working from Dornoch to The Mound. At the head of the daily mixed train, the locomotive's leading driving axle broke, and although a wheel came off, the engine managed to stay on the rails. There were, happily, no casualties amongst passengers, crew or linesiders but the event meant doom for the little tank and it was withdrawn in January. As an emergency measure BR Standard Cl.2MT 2-6-0s had been passed to work the branch the year before when the raising of the axle limit was granted up to fourteen tons maximum under a BTC Light Railway (Amendment) Order. The use of the ex CR 0-4-4T in previous years was something of a gamble which paid off because their axle loading was just over seventeen tons! The turning of blind eyes comes to mind. To replace the Highland tank working the Dornoch branch on a more permanent basis, the Scottish Region raised a few eyebrows when it borrowed a Western Region 0-6-0 pannier tank, No.1646, from Croes Newydd shed in February 1957. Although No.55053 had been condemned in early January, it had taken some weeks to find a suitable replacement - the search had certainly ranged far and wide. No.55053 was due to be conveyed to Kilmarnock for scrapping in January and had even been loaded onto a suitable wagon but the said vehicle was then required for another job connected with the Dounreay development and a trip to Thurso. The tank was still inside Lochgorm works in late May minus all wheels and it was not scrapped until February 1958.

This is the Dornoch terminus in July 1955. Opened Monday 2nd June 1902, the line was at first worked by an 0-6-0 'Lochgorm' tank No.56 which was previously named BALNAIN but was then appropriately renamed DORNOCH. The two 0-4-4T 'Puggies' came new in 1905 and relieved the 0-6-0T. Having 'Light Railway' status, the line had a supposed maximum axle loading of twelve tons but as we have seen that was obviously exceeded whenever circumstances arose. The little 0-4-4Ts each used to work the branch for a fortnight at a time, the other engine 'resting' at Helmsdale. Inverness beckoned every four months for a longer examination but other wise these engines had a tranquil life on the railway. The HR tanks (even No.56) always worked the branch running chimney first to The Mound whereas the exWR tank No.1646 did the opposite (typically) running bunker first. No.1646 was later joined by sister No.1649 and No.55236 returned to Thurso. The engine shed remained intact throughout the life of the branch (I suppose fifty-eight years is not too long) with no recorded detrimental incidents. Note the large pile of discarded timber alongside the engine shed - enough there for a week or two at Crewe North I should imagine. In amongst that pile, possibly, was a timber snowplough or the remains of which, at one time, could be attached to the front bufferbeam of the branch engine whenever circumstances deemed it necessary. In later years (BR days) it seems to have fallen out of use and ended up in a firebox. The driver, and supposedly his fireman did too, rented a cottage near to the coaling stage, out of picture to the left. The coaling stage itself was rarely used, the crew instead pulling the engine alongside a full wagon and shovelling coal directly into the bunker. All the point changing within the terminus was performed from a ground frame situated where the photographer is standing. This place closed in June 1960 taking with it a piece of British rural railway history the likes of which we will never see again. 57

Heading back to Inverness a call was made at Dingwall again that day. The trio were in time to see this evening arrival from Kyle of Lochalsh with Cl.5 No.44719 in charge. Nicely lined out, the 4-6-0 had not long been out of St Rollox shops but was already sporting a coating of grime. The vehicle behind the tender appears to be the Engineers saloon. The Strathpeffer branch trains terminated here, in a bay at the north end of the Down platform just beyond the road bridge near the rear of this train. The timetable was arranged to have trains for the various routes arriving and departure in a close sequence so as to keep passenger connection waiting times down to a minimum. So Dingwall would have a short period of intense activity followed by long periods of quiet. Motive power for the branch was provided by Dingwall engine shed and over the years of the branch's existence - 1885 to 1946 - the motive power was both varied and somewhat unusual. Besides the usual Highland offerings prior to Grouping, and afterwards, the LMS introduced at various times an ex London & North Western 0-6-2T, a Sentinel steam railcar, and a G&SW 0-4-4T. In the last decade the branch services were handled by six-coupled tender engines.

On the shed No.54458 (now facing the opposite way to this morning's pose) had been joined by No.54493 (which had been banking on the Kyle line) and an unidentified Stanier Class 5. The place was quiet now - had it ever been any different - anyway it appears everything was ready to pass through the night hours without change although there was no sign of the 0-4-4T which had been shunting earlier.

Inverness, Highland Railway. Probably one of the most spectacular engine sheds in the country, from a visual point of view, especially from this vantage point. Its perfect symmetry and grand entrance should have been preserved for all time - what a base this could have been for all those railtours around Scotland, all the preserved Stanier Class 5's could have been stabled here along with others - but it was a missed opportunity. Nowadays buildings can be 'Listed' by anyone to ensure future survival but back in the 1960's when this place became vacant - no longer required - all people wanted was modernisation, or so we were told. 'Out with the old, in with the new.' Securing this place to give future enthusiasts an inkling, for instance, of the kind of capital expenditure required to stable and service steam locomotives, should have been a priority.

But let us remember that the preservationist movement was in its infancy then, saving a steam locomotive for a few thousand pounds was a monumental undertaking at the time so trying to purchase this place with its facilities and its immediate surroundings would have been beyond the imagination of most enthusiasts - we were not encourage to think big. However, within a few short years of this depot being demolished in 1963, a couple of engine sheds were secured for preservation and further use by steam locomotives - Carnforth and Didcot come to mind and latterly Barrow Hill became another preserved edifice of the age of steam - a great opportunity was lost here in the decade of modernisation and change. Perhaps the opportunity never arose?

Early morning, Friday 8th July 1955. Our final day in the Highlands. Time for one more visit to Inverness roundhouse. The shed pilot is busy moving stores, engines have been replenished with water and coal and stabled ready for their next duty - its business as usual at 60A. The 'Pug' or 'Tankie' as they were called at Inverness, was one of two Drummond CR 0F saddletanks allocated to the shed at this time, the other being No.56038 a replacement for another of its type, No.56010, which had been withdrawn from 60A in March 1950. By the summer of 1959 both of the 0-4-0STs had gone for scrap so they were not around to see the decline which took place at Inverness at the breathtaking speed it did in those first few years of the 60's.

Although wearing a 62B shedplate on Friday 8th July 1955, LMS 2P No.40600 was part of the Kittybrewster allocation and had been for more than a year. It appears that Kittybrewster shed was either short of 61A shedplates or that the 4-4-0 was possibly on loan but given the latter alternative, shed plates were usually fitted. However, the simple fact remains that the engine was definately on the books at 61A whilst still carrying a Dundee plate. Besides working in this part of Scotland during the period under review - Kittybrewster had six of them - many of the ex LMS 2P class resident on the old South-western' lines attended Inverurie works for maintenance whenever St Rollox could not accommodate them. This particular engine started life on the old Midland lines and by late 1935 was working from Millhouses shed. At Nationalisation it was at Stranraer until transferred to Dundee in October 1952. In April 1954 Kittybrewster became its home until October 1956 when a move to Keith shed was to be its last until withdrawn in April 1959. After a year in open store (awaiting a buyer) at Ferryhill shed it was purchased by Motherwell Machinery & Scrap Co. in early 1960.

Considering this BR Standard Cl.4 tank had been allocated to Kittybrewster shed since October 1954, it is surprising to see that No.80106 still did not have a shedplate in this 8th July 1955 photograph (see previous caption re 40600). There isn't even a legend on the bufferbeam except to state it was Class 4 - perhaps 61A could not believe their luck and were not going to stretch it applying shedplates. These 2-6-4Ts first came to Aberdeen in October 1951 in the shape of No.80020. It was joined a month later by No.80021, another Brighton product, which was then joined in January 1952 by Nos.80028 and 80029, both new, ex Brighton. They had been sent north to replace the ageing D40 and D41 4-4-0s which were fast disappearing from the Kittybrewster allocation. The Cl.4 tanks carried out the same duties as the former GNSR engines but had a slight problem with water capacity on the longer turns, otherwise they were welcomed by the 61A enginemen because not only could they perform but they yielded footplate comfort which was previously only dreamt about. Out of sequence Nos.80004 and 80005 arrived in November 1952 for long stints at Kittybrewster. Next came Doncaster-built Nos.80106 to 80109 which joined them in October and November 1954 - just in time for the winter services again! No.80110 should have got to Aberdeen in November but it did not arrive until December having been borrowed on the way by York and later Tweedmouth depots. It was reported that these latter engines had a recess in the left side of the cab sidesheet to fit the Manson tablet exchanger which was still in use on this section of BR but the cut-out was so well executed it was difficult to see from certain angles, however, it can just be made out on No.80106 beneath the driver at the same level as the number. The summer of 1955 brought two more of the class, Nos.80121 and 80122, which were sent off to Keith from Kittybrewster in November for winter service. However, 1957 brought a change in fortune and three of Kittybrewster's allocation were sent to Polmadie. In the early 1960's five more started work on the former GNSR metals with both Kittybrewster and Keith sheds getting the benefit of them but to balance out these movements 61A and its sub had to give up some of their Standard tanks.

J36 No.65213 had led something of a charmed life since coming into traffic in November 1889. To give it an extension of life the NBR rebuilt it in 1914 when it was already thirty-five years old. At Grouping it worked from Kipps shed but moved over to Parkhead shortly afterwards. In January 1942 it was sent away to Borough Gardens shed on Tyneside and after there moved up to Tweedmouth in March 1943. In September of that year it was sent to Stirling and a month later transferred to Thornton Junction shed. To finish off 1943 it was reallocated to Perth in December. In April 1950 Ferryhill shed beckoned and finally in November 1952 Kittybrewster required its services. In the April before this July visit, the 0-6-0 had undergone a Light Intermediate at Inverurie and the pensioner looks all the better for it. In October 1956 the engine had one final repair which was carried out at Kittybrewster shed in the old workshop there. Condemnation occurred on 10th April 1957 and shortly afterwards it was sent to Kilmarnock works for cutting up. Oh, I forgot to mention that in May 1939 this engine, then numbered 9622, was withdrawn for scrapping but because of the sudden onset of war it was re-instated at the end of August after a General overhaul.

In their quest for the exotic and rare, Keith and friends had to visit Aberdeen to get sight of the pair of Z4 tank engines, Nos.68190 and 68191, which had spent virtually the whole of their lives working on the former GNSR metals around Aberdeen. Although not withdrawn until April 1960 and March 1959, from July 1954 onwards the pair were to spend long periods in store, under cover at Kittybrewster shed, and therefore unreachable for photographers. Luckily for our intrepid trio both engines were active in early July 1955 as witness No.68191 here at Kittybrewster. On 14th July No.68190 went back into store until 27th August whilst No.68191 went into works for its last overhaul on 26th August not emerging from Inverurie until 7th October. The storage periods thereafter got longer, many during the summer months so our friends were lucky indeed to 'bag' this one. The pair of similar Z5's were even more elusive with one on shed out of use, No.68192, whilst the other, No.68193, was in a nine month long hibernation.

N15 class No.69201 stands gleaming over the ashpit at Kittybrewster on Friday 8th July 1955, just a week after completing a Light Intermediate overhaul at Inverurie works - 14th June to 1st July 1955. By now allocated to Ferryhill shed, arriving there in December 1949 from Dunfermline, the ex LNER (North British Railway) 0-6-2T appears to have had a repaint during its time in works. The successful N15 class numbered ninety-nine engines which were complimented with a further six N14 class from which the N15 had derived. Built between 1910 and 1924, the class was constructed by outside contractors and Cowlairs works, however, the latter workshop did not get involved with their manufacture until after the LNER took over. No.9227 (69224) of that Cowlairs batch was the last locomotive built at the workshop, coming into traffic on 5th April 1924. No.69201 was one the class built in March 1923 by R.Stephenson & Co. and was sent to work at Dunfermline. Its first General overhaul was carried out between 3rd June and 30th September 1925 at Darlington. Thereafter Cowlairs became responsible for its maintenance until wartime when it visited Inverurie a couple of times. After a 'General' at Inverurie in February 1947 it returned to Cowlairs care until it moved to Aberdeen in December 1949. Thereafter Inverurie took over. On 16th December 1957 No.69201 was transferred to the former GNSR shed at Keith but on the tenth day of the following month it was condemned. By March 1958 it was being cut up at Kilmarnock works.

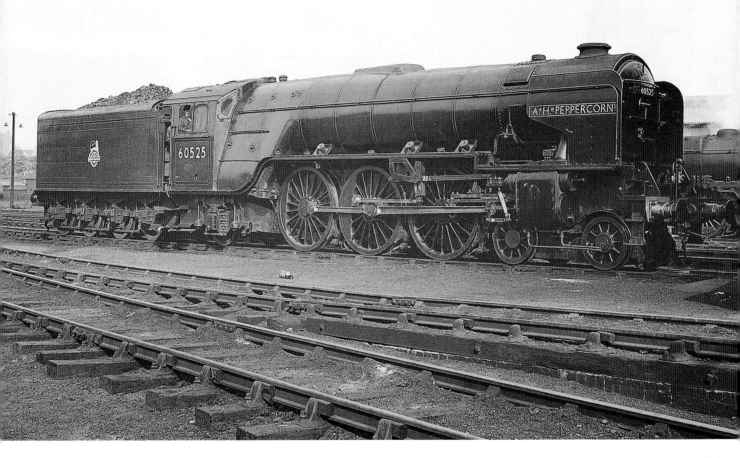

The final visit of Friday took in Ferryhill shed where Pacifics were expected and found. This is Peppercorn A2 and class leader No.60525 A.H.PEPPERCORN looking resplendent even though its last works visit had been in November 1954. The depot took a pride in this engine which they acquired in August 1949 after its first General overhaul and when it was renumbered at Doncaster works. There was three of these Peppercorn Pacifics shedded at Aberdeen Ferryhill at this time, No.60531 BAHRAM had arrived just a couple of weeks earlier than No.60525 on 7th August 1949 and was to leave in December 1962. The other was No.60532 BLUE PETER which arrived in January 1951 for a ten year stint, after which it departed for Dundee, only to return to 61B on 4th December 1966 ready to be sold later that month for preservation. No.60525 left Ferryhill in April 1963 for St Rollox works Glasgow where it was to be broken up. The condemnation had taken place on Wednesday 27th March. Other 'Big' engines allocated to Ferryhill at this time in 1955 included ten Gresley V2. Of course more ex LNER Pacifics were to grace the yard here during the last years of steam working in Scotland. The Gresley A4's had their swansong working the three-hour Glasgow expresses from Aberdeen, a fitting end to a fitting class of locomotive.

After spending the night in Aberdeen, Keith and his compatriots took a last look around Kittybrewster on Saturday 9th July prior to setting off southwards. Their detour to 61A was not in vain as this St Margarets based D30, No.62421 LAIRD O'MONKBARNS graced the shed yard and was nicely positioned for a photograph. The 4-4-0 had just completed its last General overhaul at Inverurie and was now 'running-in' prior to working back to Edinburgh. As can be seen the engine and tender are fully lined and the bufferbeam sports the legend D30 in true Inverurie style. The D30 would go back into traffic and enjoy another five years of work before being called into Cowlairs in July 1960 for the inevitable 'chop'. However, in 1955 the new decade was some time away, it seemed, and this forty-one year old locomotive would pose many more times for the camera - albeit never in this condition again.

Just down the yard and in complete contrast to the D30, was this named K2 No.61790 LOCH LOMOND. The 2-6-0 was a newcomer to Kittybrewster and had only been there a year and one month, hence the lack of shedplate (see earlier captions re this subject). Named since December 1933, the K2 had spent most of its life working on the West Highland line being allocated to either Eastfield or Fort William. It appears to be in dire need of a clean or more likely a overhaul and the latter is what it was waiting for because on 6th August it was accepted into Cowlairs for a General repair. Note the lack of a front coupling, no doubt a breakage of sorts had occurred. Note also the lubrication lines positioned beneath the boiler handrail in their own conduit. The K2 class first came to Kittybrewster in September 1952 when 61793 appeared two months later Nos. 61779, 61782, and 61792 arrived from the West Highland. In June 1954 Nos.61783 and 61790 were the next aboard whilst in July No.61734 went directly to Keith and was quickly followed by 61789, 61782, 61792 and 61793. All five worked out their days at 61C until withdrawal. Meanwhile No.61790 was kept at 61A and that engine had company in the form of 61741 from March 1957. Both engines stayed at Kittybrewster until condemned.

Forfar, Angus. En route from Aberdeen to Dundee on that last day, the trio called in to view the situation at Forfar engine shed at about midday. This former Caledonian locomotive depot was opened in December 1899 to replace an earlier shed dating from 1850. The shed was a brick built four road, double-ended affair, complete with coaling stage and turntable. In BR days it was coded 63C whereas the LMS had it down as 29D with three sub sheds at Arbroath, Brechin, and Alyth in Perthshire. The allocation of Forfar in 1935 consisted six McIntosh 2P 0-4-4T, one McIntosh 3F 0-6-0T, six Drummond 2F 'Jumbo' 0-6-0 tender engines and three Pickersgill 3F 0-6-0 tender engines - note all were ex Caley. By Nationalisation the number of engines allocated had risen somewhat to twenty-three with three McIntosh and Pickersgill 3P 4-4-0s taking the place of three 0-6-0s. The 0-4-4T count had gone up to thirteen whilst three newcomers, in the shape of the Hughes/Fowler 'Crab', had arrived in 1946. No.42738 was the last arrival and came onto the property in September. In this July 1955 view the engine is stabled outside the east end of the shed alongside the turntable and has another three years to serve at 63C before moving to Hamilton in October 1958. The other two 2-6-0s, No.42800 and 42801 arrived a bit earlier and came together from Kingmoor via Perth in July 1946. No.42801 stayed at Forfar until November 1958 when it returned to Perth. On the other hand No.42800 came and went between Perth and Forfar during 1955, 56, 57 and finally in July 1958 left Forfar for good, going to Perth.

We end our week long trek through Scotland at Dundee Tay Bridge engine shed. to round things off there is another little gem in the can, Y9, No.68123 complete with tender. Although the tender is as dirty as the engine and markings are either faint or non-existent, it was actually Wagon No.971563 which was registered as Departmental Stock belonging to the Motive Power Department and marked LOCO DEPT DUNDEE. Its weight was 5 tons 9 cwt. and it had been coupled to the 'Pug' since June 1953 after the engine had a Light Intermediate overhaul at Cowlairs. The conical spark arrester over the chimney was an extra precaution fitted to those engines which shunted around the docks area at Dundee where bales of jute were constantly landed. During the late summer of 1957 the former Caledonian engine shed at Dundee West started to receive the first of a new batch of the North British Loco. Co. built diesel hydraulic 0-4-0s and by November ten of them had taken over the workings formerly carried out by the Y9. A lone diesel from the same company, numbered 11703 (later D2703), had been the pathfinder for this class having arrived in Dundee during August 1955 to prove their worth. In December 1957 'Pug' No.68123 moved on to pastures anew at Kipps. Having undergone a 'General' just eleven months before, there was still plenty of fight in the old dog and it went on working until the summer of 1960 when the inevitable took place. It was cut up at its birthplace - Cowlairs - aged sixty-one years. Note the coal piled high in the tender of the Stanier Cl.5 behind the 0-4-0 - that must have been exceeding the loading gauge.